ANCHOR BOOKS

Sunny Moments

Edited by

Sarah Andrew

First published in Great Britain in 2002 by
ANCHOR BOOKS
Remus House,
Coltsfoot Drive,
Peterborough, PE2 9JX
Telephone (01733) 898102

HB ISBN 1 85930 110 X
SB ISBN 1 85930 112 6

FOREWORD

Anchor Books is a small press, established in 1992, with the aim of promoting readable poetry to as wide an audience as possible.

The poems presented here have been selected from many entries. Editing proved to be a difficult task and as the Editor, the final selection was mine.

I trust this selection will delight and please the authors and all those who enjoy reading poetry.

Sarah Andrew
Editor

CONTENTS

Isle Of Dreams

Come with me to my Isle of Dreams
Where the mountains reach the sky.
Laughing streams hurry down the hill
And the hungry seagulls cry.

Come in spring when the cuckoos sing
And lambs are gambolling free.
Come at night when the stars are bright
And the moon rides on the sea.

Feel the thrill as you climb the hill
For I know how you will feel -
Such surprise, but believe your eyes
For this paradise is real.

Rise at dawn when the day is born
And birds are waking their young.
Then you will hear the sweetest song
That ever has been sung.

Isle of Dreams, oh my Isle of Dreams
Where I'll always long to be.
Yet still by far the best of all
Is that you'll be there with me.

Carol Ratcliffe

NEIGHBOURHOOD - ME

decided to move on, better myself
away from our road
which usually looks clean on a monday
after the binmen have been
they deserve a medal, they really do

when the removal van came
her, next-door, knocked, didn't barge in
her daughter had a baby boy, 5lbs 2oz
they might be getting married now
invited to the wedding, of course

the old lady, over the road
is 80 on sunday
her son is coming for 3 months
from australia
must remember to send her a card

the nice catholic woman
forget her name, irish, artistic
offered to bake a special birthday cake
with golden roses and pink icing

maggie will be there for the knees up
and her daughter
the one with the pink and green hair, spiky
passed her a levels last week
can't be on crack after all, can she?

they are building a new youth centre, at last
billy's mum will be pleased
worries herself sick about him
no job
on street corners all day and all night
up to no good

poor mrs smith's husband died, a blessing really
she doesn't think so, of course
the older neighbours have drawn the curtains
he was such a nice man, he really was

mind you, this morning, on my new doorstep
fumbling for the key, as always
my new neighbour, next door
rushed straight past, not a word
shutting her front door with a bang

she completely forgot to smile at me

Alfa

The Precious Stones Of Memory

Beautiful things remembered and magic times recalled
Are like precious stones, dropped idly here and there,
In fields by riversides, in winding country lanes,
Like faded rosebuds, or a ribbon from her hair.

As I retrace my footsteps along the road of memory,
I pick up a thousand gems I long since left behind.
And as I find each gleaming stone I hold it safe,
And hide it in the secret places of my mind.

Some I find are broken and gone beyond recall,
Or turned into useless baubles of powdered rock and clay.
But many will make a shiny golden necklace
Of memories, to keep and treasure along life's leaf-strewn way.

Win Wilcock

My Teddy

Teddy you're always there
sitting on that faded chair

But I love you that's all I care
as I rock you in my cradle of love.

You were there for my first tooth, first walk,
first toothache when I got the pain
and the terrible days of cold again.

I turned to you when I got a smack
because I knew you wouldn't answer back.

You were there in storms of night
which gave me howls of fright.

When I got chicken pox, when I got the flu,
when I was too frightened to go the loo.

When we moved you were there
sitting in the removal chair.

But now you are a terrible mess,
just look how you're dressed.
One eye missing, where's your fur?
I still want you and that's how I care.

Jay

EVENING

The evening draws near,
As traffic is bestilled,
Becoming silent
  - hard to hear.

As evening draws closer,
With fewer people abroad
And footpaths empty
  - the street lights flare.

Evening changes to night
Reviving coexisting anew
And nightlife bustles
  - society thaws true.

Gary J Finlay

Me

I'm tall and slim good looking too
My beauty lies deep inside so true
Writing my poetry so all the world can see
Tells what beauty inside really means to me
This is a way I can tell the world what I want to say
As all my special words come day by day
Speak your mind just be true
Being happy your whole life through
Make your mind up, you have nothing to lose
Some people are unlucky they don't get chance to choose
Take a step back, look at yourself from inside
Follow your heart be full of pride
Remember none of us are perfect in this land
Take to your inner soul and make a stand
Be healthy, romantic exciting not dull
Don't forget, look inside your soul, beauty is skin deep
It's not just here today it's here for keeps
When you are fed up and had enough
Just say, 'Oh that's tough.'
Life's too short soon comes to an end
Count your blessings speak to a friend
Have a life long happiness here and now
Pick yourself up, *do it now!*

Good Luck, Take Care

Anne Davey

BEYOND BURDENS

The best things in life are free
And I am not the first to see.
So how come people choose to buy
And fill their lives with hue and cry?

I've seen fools fight for matters small
And still, they got nowhere at all.
Just stress and strain and pressure pain
To suffer over and again.

Accumulating worldly wealth
And often at the cost of health.
Yet never really knowing why
Except to leave it when they die.

Who understands the men who strive?
For all they gain outlives their lives.
They go without a single claim
Who dies as rich, dies rich in shame.

Such petty worries do we bear
Because of such, small ties were care.
Securities, insurances,
Such paradox endurances.

For nought's secured, nought insured
For nought in life is so assured.
Accumulation equals strife
As most have fallen foul of life.

Though you must buy, buy what you need
Let yearnings temper not your greed.
The one free thing that stands above
Makes all things free when borne with love.

Gemini Cherry

SUMMER'S PLAY

The sound of bees,
And 'neath the trees
Carpet, daisy sprinkled.
Ceiling of leaves,
The willow grieves,
Sparkling waters twinkled.

Foxglove drooping,
Wild rose stooping
Where the pathway parted.
Doves soft cooing
Senses wooing,
Swift the swallow darted.

Birds full of life
Chirpings are rife,
Many young ones to feed.
Squirrels alert
Bright eyed and pert,
Climbing branches with speed.

Bushes flowering,
Petals showering
On rivers of bluebells.
Hedgerows glow bright,
Hawthorn snow white,
Sweet scent in woods and dells.

I sit and gaze
Lost in a haze
Of garden's wondrous charms.
Could I stay long,
Away from the throng,
All nature fear disarms.

Evelyn Balmain

FAVOURITE THINGS

My two little kittens,
are among my favourite things,
watching their little antics
and the laughter which it brings.

Then there is the gold ring,
mother bought me at twenty-one.
It's a little worn and tarnished,
yet I'm saving it for my son.

I mustn't forget the memories,
which can never be taken away,
whether happy, sad, or transcendent,
they're always here to stay.

Yet again there's the grandiose woodland,
we visited come rain or showers,
holding hands with mother
and picking such glorious flowers.

I think my favourite's my mother,
such a precious gift of love.
Such a kind, caring guardian
could only be sent from above.

Steve Kettlewell

SUNSET SNOWFLAKE

The time has come for the sun to set.
Colours disappear darkness is upon us.
The glistening colours are no longer there,
All that glistens is a single snowflake.

Flittering, fluttering, floating down,
A sweet soft breeze is blowing around.
The snowflake lands upon my brow,
No more little snowflakes floating down.

Carly Lancaster

Lavender Oil And Warm Milk

Why use addictive sleeping pills
People think they can cure insomnia's ills
When it comes to wind down at night
People keep the pill box in sight
But there's no need to go to the brink
The solution is more natural than you think
The milk is in your fridge
Just warmed in a mug
Is better sipped slowly and rivals any drug
Lavender oil drops on the pillowcase is best
To help you have a natural night's rest.

Pauline Edwards

Gone By

I like the old things and the old way of life
All troubles seemed small, some little strife
Soon were forgotten by love and attention
To be hard up was not worth the mention
There wasn't too much to spoil your choice
How small were the gifts that we did rejoice
All neighbours were friends
All strangers were liked
If one was to fight the wrong was put right
Everyone cared and cared not less
Slow to condemn and quick to bless
Life now is a drag also so sad
It's hard to find someone that makes you feel glad
How I long for the days that have gone by
I wallow in memories to laugh and to cry
I wish those days back that have faded away
And I faded too I am glad to say.
I can't live in a world that's now deranged
Hello and goodbye life starts and it ends
It goes on in its time and compatibly blends.

A B Lawson

My Treasure

The one I cherish most, is my mother
I do not like to boast, but there is no other
- like her

She is the diamond in the crown
The one of most renown
- though she is not famous

She gives me unconditional love
Taught I'm sure by the Spirit above
Never complains, even when in pain
Witty, intelligent, she can be cheeky too
Gentle, resilient, her love shines through
- in everything she does

When I'm hurting, she is always there
To pick me up when I'm in despair
Her common sense attitude helps get me through
The bad times and I tell you it is true
that a Mother knows best.
As for all the rest
There would be too many books to write
and not enough time
Her life speaks volumes
- she is one of a kind.

Suffice to say her character was formed by a hard life
She was of the 'old school' and poverty was rife
She raised five children all alone
we never starved, and her love always shone
to get us through and now we are all grown
A credit to her determination and sheer love, alone.

And now in her autumn years, she is rich in our adoration
She has peace and enjoyment, and helps with the preparation
To put our children through the school of life
She is wise to show them to appreciate the rainbows,
as well as the hard knocks and the strife.

Yes, she is the treasure I will cherish for all time
I thank God I have been so blessed with a mother like mine.

Mary A Shovlin

A Special Friend

A gentle hand stroking my head,
Soothing words being said,
Plenty of food for me to eat,
Someone to bathe my old, sore feet.
I'm eight years old and going grey,
My new mum says that I can stay,
She says I'm ill so I must rest,
I'll have a sleep, my mum knows best.
My life's been hard and now I'm shattered
I need my rest 'cause I've been battered,
It feels so strange to have a home,
Where I am kissed and never alone.
I'm loved and hugged, my future's bright,
I'll sleep with Mum in bed tonight,
For months I've slept out in the cold,
It's too much when you're getting old.
But now I'm safe and cared for too,
There's so many things I'd like to do,
Like go for walks or play with toys,
At my age I'm not into boys.
There are lots of greyhounds here, you see
Who are too old to home, just like me,
So we're staying here until the end,
With Mum, our very special friend.

Pat Bradley

Also Laphraoig

Hail to Thee, blithe Spirit, hanging suspended,
Bum upwards, pointing towards the roof,
Nose downward, temptingly upended,
Your contents golden and a hundred proof.

Steep barley in burn water from the hill.
Malt in a kiln. Mix grist with water in a vat.
Ferment for several hours. Add yeast. Distil.
Mature for fifteen years in bourbon casks. And that

Is that. Ambrosia, the liquor of the gods,
May thrill your supernatural drinking school. In
Scotland, however, ichor from peaty sods,
We opt for Bruichladdich, Lagavulin.

Watter o'life! Scots cannae get enough
O' yon archetypal nectar, *usquebaugh!*

Norman Bissett

LOST MAGIC

My childhood winters had a magic all their own.
Where has that magic gone?
Muffled in woolly scarves and warm hand-knitted gloves
We snowballed, sledged and snowmen built,
Working away for hours on end
With cheeks all red and glowing.

The milkman with horse and cart loaded with shining churns
Called at the kitchen door
Pouring the creamy milk into our waiting jugs
For porridge hot to warm us for the day.

As dusk closed in, with curtains drawn
We'd sit before the fire, long toasting forks held out
Spearing the bread and crumpets
Lavishly to be spread with melting, golden butter.

On cold and frosty nights, we gathered, lanterns held on high,
To sing our carols joyously along the village lanes,
To end up at the Manor House for hot drinks and mince pies:
Then sleepily we'd wend our way back to our welcome beds.

We made our own amusements - the many games we played,
Ludo and Snakes and Ladders were my favourites, I recall.
The books we read, the painting books, the simple toys we loved,
The spinning tops, the dolls, Meccano for the boys.

A different time, a different world,
Where has that magic gone?

The children of this century prefer to stay indoors,
They crouch for hours on winter nights (and in the summer too)
Before the TV or their own computer screens,
And if they venture out sometimes, where is it that they go?

They haunt the shops, they stand around, with no real aim in sight,
And as they're bored and know not what to do,
They vandalise or turn to drugs,
To pass the long and weary hours -
So much enjoyment missing from their lives.

They've lost the magic, lost their childhood,
Where has that magic gone?

Roma Davies

A Child's Dream

To live and dream in rainbow sunsets
The transfusion between mind and reality
The colours sunburnt onto my retina
To run screaming from the burning corn fields
And rolling naked in the mud.

To climb the ivory towers
To fight my enemies with silver swords
And waltz across marble floors
To kiss the softest, ruby lips
To play in the funeral pyre.

To believe in fairies and Father Christmas
To run a minute mile
Sleep in everglade forests
To hear my mother's lullabies
'Oh sweet child, this is life!'

R H Whiting

HELEN

Helen is so special to her mum and me
She suffers from learning difficulties
And Helen is so special
She makes you understand by little points
with her hands
Although she's an adult, she's like a little girl
She likes to go shopping or home with Mum
But she's never glum
Many operations she's been through
but she's never blue
Her courage I'd like just half an ounce
She understands what you're saying
Every bit
And she's been so lucky when she's been sick
Quite a little fighter
Doesn't give up
That's why we love her so much.

L Bevan

CHEERFUL?

Get up and wander the world,
see people's lives become unfurled,
keep that smile on your face,
open your heart and be embraced.

I don't believe in destiny or truth,
for it is all wasted in your youth.
I don't believe in miracles or love,
for it will be thrown to the stars above.
All you need to do is follow your heart,
then you and happiness won't be far apart.

Wake up and say hello to everyone,
look out of the window of freedom,
and shout out 'What a lovely day,'
and make sure they hear what you say.

I don't believe in fate or gold,
for it is only what you behold.
I don't believe in faith or fealty,
for it is only what they want you to be.
All you need is a kind, thoughtful mind,
then you can have the happiness you find.

Stand up and sing out a song,
make some other people sing along,
make it a happy and melodic tune,
then everyone will be singing it soon.

(Smile every once in a while and
find a different kind of happiness).

Dale Mullock

OUR GROUP

Sitting in armchairs so cosily
Molly And Evelyn, Norman and me,
Doris and Lyn and Doris again,
Perhaps 'tis better that I explain.

We have no partners, we live alone,
We're folk who could have so lonely grown,
So we treasure each others company,
We've almost become a family.
Gathering in Christian fellowship,
Playing some old game, or going for a trip,
Sharing our food whether snack or meal,
Making the teachings of Christ so real,
As in each others homes we gather,
In Christ give thanks to our Heavenly Father.

Alan Ellsmore

Cares

I'm so besotted with love,
I cannot explain,
It comes like a shallow mist,
Wisps cover like a dusty sheen,

The more I think of you, the more it gathers,
Closing around warm and comforting,
Like a long forgotten memory,
Dream so reassuring loving comfort,

I have succumbed to you in thought
like a dog baying at the moon,

Burbling and bumbling through sentences
of thought, can I bridge a gap,
Walking quietly talking of things,
So much in common and yet no ties,
The mist covers the ground no lies,

I crave your thoughts and emotions,
What do you know of me?
Love long lasting shrouded in mist,
Craving affection come closer,
Craving, loving you appear,
The mist is no more.

K M Clemo

Lasting Love

Lying here together,
Our bodies all entwined,
Feeling rather sleepy
After being wined and dined.
We snuggle up together,
All my worries drift away
And I know I'll still love you
When I'm old and grey.
You've always been there for me,
I can't finish this affair,
I'm afraid it is impossible
To give up my teddy bear.

Marlene Parmenter

SILENT MOON

Struck by the moon into a silence.
An ashen globe, giving all prisms of sinister light.
Shadows grab at me with talons and fingers;
All is cloaked in darkness and fear of the night.

The pale glow, at once insubstantial
Yet devious, hideous and tinged with remorse.
Lichen grows on tombstones, somehow radiant,
Obliquely, mists of time outline my course.

Struck by the moon into a silence,
Always winter overgrows this moss of memory.
While the world sleeps, pour your light on my world,
And spread your cooling cloak on me.

Andrew Detheridge

The Wonder Of Toast

I ate a slice of toast
With butter, jam - so nice.
I thought 'This toast tastes good!
I'll have another slice.'

More bread went in the toaster,
And yummy toast came out;
And none could understand
Just how this came about.

And so I asked my toaster,
'I do not know,' it said.
'It's something I've not thought about,
Just ask the bread instead.'

But when I asked my slices
About this browning lark,
They same, 'Come back at midnight
And we'll tell you, when it's dark.'

And so around the midnight hour
I tiptoed from my bed,
And went into the kitchen
Where I waited for the bread.

Two slices and a crust came out
And whispered in my ear:
'It's all to do with mental stuff -
just watch awhile, my dear.'

They climbed into the toaster
And began to meditate.
They jumped out hot and nice and brown -
And so the toast I ate.

Geoff Lowe

SWEET SPRINGTIME

I'm dancing with the shadow of sunshine,
Happiness and love.
Maybe some is coming from above,
Well! It's sweet springtime,
Which is my joy and heart's delight.
Sweet songs our ears do greet,
I wonder who I'll meet.
The fields do breathe with freshness,
Sweet little daisies do kiss our feet.
While trees and blossoms fill the air,
And birds their song do sing,
In this beautiful, sweet springtime so fair.

Elisabeth Dill Perrin

Where

All alone with no one to share,
Is the way I planned to be there
A bright, golden sun in a cloudless sky,
With a babbling brook to sit by.

Peace and quiet all around.
What a wonderful place I have found.
Where is this wondrous place you ask?
Now you have set me quite a task.

For it is all in my mind you see.
I often let it wander free.
While stuck in seething traffic jam,
Boiling engine, rattling fan.
Brought back to Earth, with a yawn,
By very impatient, *motor horn!*

G W Bailey

A Summer Place

It's the reason why we return to you
as often as we can
for the peace and tranquillity
the unique release you hold in your hand
the enormity of your space
picturesque, wild and free
that jewel of a clear blue sky
reaching out as far as the eye can see
never asking, never pressing, never questioning
why you're needed so
and always accepting that there'll come a time
when we have to go.

Katherine Parker

GRANDCHILDREN

Smily faces,
Giggles and grins.
Happy are the
children we've
never seen.

Running, playing,
Learning all day.
New adventures
on the way.

Happy we are
to see them grow.
healthy and wise
we love them so.

Their smile makes
the sun shine,
Their heart gives
out a warm glow.

These are the things
that make us
love them so.

Sylvia E Clark

TREES

It's easy to pass you, with unseeing eyes.
While problems torment us, or past pleasures unwind,
So familiar you are, we oft miss all the fun,
Of watching your antics, or hear your soft sighs
when leaves turn to gold, and leave you behind
and seeds have all fallen, the complete cycle to run.

Sometimes so quiet, yet while vibrant life
Flit between branches, or up trunk swiftly run.
You rustle and stir, whispering your special way
News gathered from breezes, as they stealthily pass,
Yet this exciting to see, as in anger or strife
Your movements are fierce, as you swirl and you sway.

Oh trees, what pleasures, what life, what burdens you bear
Your branches creak, or moan as if with new fear,
Ever changing your form, when seen in a new way
In sunlight or mist, maybe dripping with rain
A new magic you have, of making my brain
See fantasies of shapes, giving new joy to each day.

You Maple I've seen, through mist in the spring
Your trunk all twisted, it has split at the base,
You looked like a dancer, standing poised on her toes
With body on the turn, as arms outward you fling,
Your gay skirts are aswirl as you turn to and fro
Shrouded in mist, where God chose your stage.

Oh Poplar too, have your own special shapes
One, sprawling and rough, with long, slender limbs,
While t'other reach up, as if claiming the sky.
Your leaves keep chattering, as if debating their fate
Knowing they must leave you, to wither and die,
From branches that reach upwards, to the God that knows why.

One tree, that for centuries has always been near
To the places where man has set up his home,
Cut to all shapes, the Yew can be found,
By castles and mansions, where your green has become dear
To masters of planning where beauty abound
And your age-long presence shade churchyards and tombs.

But I see with great sadness the stark, gaunt signs,
Where lofty Elms, lose their battle to survive
From unseen foe, starving life-blood from veins.
How lovely lanes, once shaded by branches so green,
Now echo to axes and saws angry whine,
As man tries to help by burning where beetle, has been.

But the Oak, has something the others do lack,
Being linked with 'Old England' her own lovely tree,
Majestic in shape, even when partly fallen, or having wide cracks,
The tales you could tell, as for hundreds of years
You veterans, have been watching our fight to be free,
While providing fine ships to repel all enemy attacks.

R W Knights

THE BEST THINGS IN LIFE

My best thing in life is to have a picnic outside!
And enjoy life to the very best.
I am a man that lives life out
I love to walk in the countryside and admire everything
That my eyes can see!
And the wild flowers with their many lovely colours.
Especially if the weather is nice
Nothing is better in life than having a picnic out
What can be better?
The children play and us parents enjoy the day.
In the open air.
This is the best thing in life.
That I will never be tired of
Eating and drinking with good friends
Making our life more perfect
And the best thing in life is a picnic outside.

Antonio Martorelli

Joyful Expectations

Thanks, thanks for the mate,
A gift sent by fate,
Two cherubs as well,
In love to excel.

Help me them guide,
In peace to abide
No more lost, to roam:-
A wife and a home.

Souls dressed in Your light,
A love song to write,
A blessing, a Psalm,
To shield us from harm.

O Lord bless our bread,
May we Thy truth wed,
May friends come, abound,
Make Holy Your ground.

Each day meet our need,
All united? Indeed!
Hope rings the bell,
Yes, all will be well.

Emmanuel Petrakis

TIME AND MONEY

It's important how I spend my day,
For time is money, so they say.
I'm afraid I'm inclined to fritter time,
Playing with words to make them rhyme.

Every day I have a little bet,
But with the bookie I don't get in debt.
Friends sometimes drop by for a bit of a chat;
They know I'll always put out the welcome mat.

I might decide to cook a nice meal;
It all depends on how I feel.
I'll lose myself in a book for hours,
Then wander out and sniff the flowers.

The garden gives me so much pleasure,
There's no yardstick by which I can measure.
I'll sit on the patio with a glass in my hand
Thinking, 'How pleasant, isn't life grand.'

I rarely do anything too taxing,
I just quite simply, enjoy relaxing.
I reckon my time has been well spent
But, as far as money goes, I haven't a cent.

Geraldine Parr

Life So Special

Each and every one of us say
We have had something special in our day
We all have something special to ourselves
It may even be life itself
No matter where in the world we live
Whatever life has to give
We all have special moments to review
Sometimes wanting to repeat, anew
Life can hold so many things
Recalling special moments it brings
Wherever in life we seem to be
We all look back so we can see
Just how special it can be.

Michaela W Moore

RESTFUL MOMENTS

I walked along the river bank
One bright and sunny day.
I found a spot and settled down
For a while to stay.
But something really caught my eye
Something through the trees.
Three lovely swans were cruising by
Floating on the breeze.
With heads erect that looked so proud
So white, so pure and clean.
I really felt quite privileged
Of this picture that I had seen.
Next time I go out walking
In lovely sunny weather.
I will keep an eye out
For my friends dressed in white feather.

Dorreen Read

EDGE OF NIGHT

Gold,
Evaporates through the nimbus,
With suffuse molten wings
Across the occident horizon,
Serenading the crepuscular symphony
Through nuances of oceanic apparition,
The quietude of the village
Embraced in cautious silence,
Solidarity in curious union,
As the countenance of the church clock
Bears witness to and fro,
Breaking the violence
As the bell resonates
Across the reverie of solitude.

Anthony John Ward

MAGIC DUSK

O dark magician
I don't see your trick,
Far too dark to see,
I'd best light a wick.

Blue black is your colour,
You throw on silver too,
You dazzle me with your magic,
I'm blinded by you.

You weave such a spell
In the dead of night,
Love seems more romantic
In the warm candlelight.

How do you make the stars appear?
How do you hang out the moon?
How do you make a star shoot?
Why is it over so soon?

Where do you put the sun?
Where do the clouds go?
Dusk is the greatest magician,
Night is the greatest show.

Elizabeth Newton

TRUE LOVE

My life, is full of love, and pleasure.
My husband is so kind.
He spoils me in everything with lots!
And lots! of love!
He cooks my food and makes my bed.
He does all the washing too.
He is the most perfect man.
With lots of love as well.
His health is not so clever,
He's retired with sickness too.
He is a very special man
And loves me through and through.

Heather Breadnam

I LOVE CROCHET

Whenever my tiny hands get bored
I take my little hook
And crochet something beautiful
Like a bookmark for a book.

Sometimes it is delicate
Sometimes it is not
Sometimes it is intricate
I tie myself in knots!

When I'm feeling happy
I crochet little rings
To give away as presents
My heart begins to sing.

To see their sheer enjoyment
And the happiness therein
Hello, somebody new is stirring
Here's my opportunity to win.

Another valued customer
For this enterprise of mine
I could crochet on forever
And that is really fine.

I've completed many projects
From jackets through to mats
I really love to do it
And that is really that!

Michelle Broadbent

HAPPY TO BE HERE

When you look upon your life, and what you've done
Were there storm clouds, or was it mainly sun?
Just remember seeds you sow, need both rain and sun to grow.
And reflect that you are not the only one.

So you didn't climb that mountain in Tibet!
And your novel's not been published. - Well, not yet.
And you're not a politician; did you squander your ambition
To be famous? To be known? Just don't forget -

There's a pattern in most everything we do
We're all pieces in life's jigsaw, it is true.
For another's life don't seek; but remember you're unique
And God knows the individual that is you.

Be thankful that you're living, just be happy to be here.
Give yourself a little time to think things through.
Thank the Lord for songs, and singing, for a melody that's clear
Sing out loudly - *I'm happy to be here!*

You may feel your life's been nothing and is wasted.
You may envy rich man's wine you never tasted.
But look around you, and you'll see, Nature's richness, yours for free
Then you can laugh at poor fool's gold and how you chased it.

The eagle in the sky is a king
A monarch, over all on the wing
See the future as he flies, see yourself with different eyes
Open up your heart and let it sing.

Be thankful that you're living, just be happy to be here
Give yourself a little time to think things through.
Thank the Lord for songs, and singing, for a melody that's clear
Shout out loud - *I'm just happy to be here!*

Rose Stedman

How Sweet Thou Art

Quiet stillness wraps itself around my weary body
fresh breezes sneak through open window, sweet perfumes float
effortlessly from sleepy garden beds, leaves rustle gently,
teasing flying insects, faraway whispers embrace swaying curtains.
Strange scratchy noises interrupt dozy dreamings. Suddenly wings
flutter, bouncing feathery echo towards sleepy ears. Balmy breezes
waft ghostly tossing lacy nets towards bed's restful edges. Stretching
full length, hands tucked beneath cosy pillows, dreamy thoughts, listen,
what more delights, shall this summer's evening bring?
Squabbling tomcats hiss angry remarks to each other. Buzzing creatures
touch windowpane, playing symphonies with their tiny wings.
Clinging ivies brush daintily casting phantom shadows.
Moonlight silhouettes, mirroring funny-shaped pictures as
tiny images dance from wall to wall.

Sailing clouds block out summer's clear night's sky. Cool breezes
swathe noisily rattling open windows, fraying curtains zigzag
cable wall. Raindrops pitter-patter, oozing summery smells, become
more intense. Gliding chilly winds bathe sleepy face. Freshness
fills stuffy perfumed room, turning over toward summer's rainy
sounds. Every human sense drinks passionately nature's pleasures.

Storm clouds gather, angry lashing rain pounds over window sill
swooping downwards, splashing patio stones. Thunder rumbles,
masking out all other sounds. Lightning strikes, sending flashes
crashing earthwards. Momentous bombs epilogue warm still
summer's night. Now nature's raging wrath surges, yet how natural,
how profound, awesome blind fury she sounds so wonderfully
sweet, angels' singing voices, God's clanging symbols become my
heart, my soul, my life. I slept with Mother Nature this summer's night

Ann Hathaway

The Romany Traveller

The road is long and winding, for the travellers of the night,
as stars look down to guide the way, the moon an extra light.
Old Dobbin plods on in easy gait, wheels of time pass slowly by,
man and horse in unison, journey on beneath the clear night sky.

Through leafy lanes in silent fens, they trundle on their way,
with a secluded spot in mind; a quiet place they usually stay.
As dawn breaks, the wildlife stirs, hedgerows and trees come alive,
Fenland greenery hung with mist, here the Romany ends his drive.

The rising sun peeps through the trees, the rolling mist drifts away,
and having found his secluded spot, the traveller here will stay.
First the horse is fed and watered, then tethered out to graze,
the Romany sets up his tripod, and soon the campfire will blaze.

From the beautiful old covered wagon, emerged the traveller's wife,
and soon they were eating breakfast, what a wonderful way of life.
There's work to be done throughout the day; wares have to be made,
pans to tinker and pegs to make, that's how the traveller gets paid.

Locally the lady hawks their wares, also lucky heathers she sells,
on occasions when requested, folks' fortunes she sometimes tells.
There is washing to do, provisions to buy, during this short stay,
maintain the wagon, brush the horse, and then they get underway.

Before moving off they do ensure, the site is left spotlessly clean,
but rest assured they'd leave a mark, so others know who's been.
Clip-clop, clip-clop, down the open road, to their next port of call,
the real Romany traveller, such a wonderful sight for one and all.

Wenn-The-Penn

Boys In Royal Blue

There's nothing better than a Saturday
When I watch Birmingham City play
Clad in blue they take to the pitch
People flock here, poor and rich
100 years of nothing is what they cry
Apart from a League Cup in years gone by
Why do they flatter to deceive week in, week out
Is it a curse on the club that they'd won nowt?
Still the adrenaline rushes through every pore
Hoping to see better than what's gone before
The fans deserved better down the years
Cup semi-finals ending in tears
Perhaps Lady Luck will smile one day
Bringing a trophy we all do pray.
I hope it's in my lifetime as I'm getting on
So my offspring don't have to hear
                    that nothing's been won!

Philip O'Leary

My Writing Chair

While I'm here on this chair
My problems vanish in the air
As I sit and write
Everything will be alright
Making up people and places
New characters and different faces
Anything can happen, it's all up to me
It's my choice what will be
From this chair I've been so far
Travelled to the furthest star
Just by moving my pen up and down
Can go from city to town
I can go everywhere
From the comfort of my writing chair.

Amanda Steel

My Best Things In Life

Winning the lottery
Making magic with a lover
Some folk think that the former
Automatically leads to the other!

Cruising to where the sun does not set
Gazing north beside my new bride
Or any lover if I have no wife
Canoodling on a ship so wide

But by far the best thing in my life
Is looking forward to it all
Whether it is loadsamoney or a new lover
I will soon be having a ball.

H G Griffiths

MARILYN MANSON

The words he uses
The way he sings,
The way he controls the audience,
I love everything.

His eyes so sad
Like a fallen angel,
He has the power
To excel.

I saw him live,
He spat in my face -
I was so happy
I was in my favourite place.

I listen to his music
And problems drift away,
I can see a lot of myself in him.
I think of him every day.

His face, finely chiselled
Makes me want him so,
His body is irresistible.
I have no chance, this I know!

Jodie McKane

THE SUSSEX DOWNS

Stand on the plain
and view them
smooth hills running
east and west,
sheep dot the sides
of The Trundle
white cloudlets
shadow the rest -

Sussex Downs standing
sentinel true!

And so Blake viewed them
and wondered who else
had seen them too!
So he penned 'Jerusalem'
to ask us: In ancient time
was it true that Jesus
walked these Downs . . .?

Now the view is the same
for all of us - but the
feet are just me and you.

Michael Rowson

Roses

Rose petals loose against their own beauty
Blush pink in knowledge of their perfection,
And even though the stem gives reminder of the thorn
A fortune would I give
For a plot to grow them in that they might live,
For the sole reason
Of renewing the ancient story
Of glory reborn
With every flowering season.

Pat Isiorho

HAPPY 2002

We are all so happy, that the new year will soon arrive -
As through weeks of dark and cold days, we certainly needed to strive.
Because we know the lovely weather, and light nights will soon
be here -
We are so used to this happening continually every year.
There is good and bad throughout all lives, living here on Earth,
And the good times always compensate, and this gives life great worth.
Let's hope the new year 2002, will be free from devastations -
Like what happened in the USA, and many more locations.
It is time for all mankind, to be good to one another -
And then the world will be so great, when at last it does recover.

Elizabeth Jones (Betty)

I Love To . . .

I love to walk without any shoes,
listen to music and sing the blues.
Soak in the sun, lazily lying,
watch birds overhead, soaring, flying.
Ride on my motorbike, going fast.
Swimming at leisure, bubble baths.
Playing with my children, smiling and laughing.
Going to discos, singing and dancing.
Loving family and friends in a special way.
Watch the sun rise and set each day.
Beaches, breezes, dreams, opera singing,
riding on horses, church bells ringing.
Autumn leaves cloaking the ground,
countryside flowers to be found.
Waterfalls cascading, foaming wildly,
babies gurgling, cooing mildly.
Long nails, perfect, painted brightly.
Black lacy clothes, ones pastelled lightly.
Mystical enchantments, magical things.
Wizards, witches, bright glowing rings.
Writing, reading books of all kinds,
brave people, strong, knowing their minds.
True, kind friends, honest admiring,
forests and woods, exploring and climbing.
Animals and people, life and love.
My husband and children, our dear Lord above.

Patricia Grimsted

FRESH AIR

I find myself wandering out in the open
The air so fresh on a nice cool day,
'Let God be praised.'
Almighty Father, what a gift
When your air is pure
No cig smells, no nasty sniffs
Of anything unkempt - gone bad,
Just your pure open air so clean,
Thank you Father as I wander on
For many sights I've seen.
The robin in a bush so sweet,
Fresh water that came from the tap
That ran down upon my feet.
Cool and happy, I wander on,
Finding peace in your valley
Like eventide song.
Rings of roses doing fine
Above the lark doth fly
Sweet Father of all fresh days
That you let me wander through,
I thank you for your pure gift
Of air that keeps us all alive,
So freely given by you.
See the lambs leap for joy
Little woolly lambs at play,
For them and pure fresh air,
    Father, I thank you today.

Marion Staddon

MILLENNIUM BRIDGE

You are so delightful and full of praise
Each angle, each view, is perfect
You are like our God Almighty
Your smile is the hope of Tyneside.

You are strong and honest
Each day with you is like a thousand stars
You are full of imagination
Your evening view is a taste of Heaven.

Kenneth Mood

God's Insurance

The TV, fridge and washer must be insured and up to date,
The house and all the property even to a damaged slate.
We take all these precautions about our material wealth,
Let's be insured, specially for our health.
Yet we have a policy where there's no cash to pay,
God's insurance, that inner peace He gives us every day.
We are a world of violence, full of racial hate and greed,
Where kidnaps and killings make for normal read.
But God's insurance is secure, it's ours to have and hold,
Now at this moment in value more than gold.
Though trials may beset us sorrows come but never harm,
When we have God's insurance, His small voice, that inner calm
He sends His peace to all the world, why hesitate and doubt?
Plunge deep down inside your soul, take God's insurance out.

Mavis Catlow

CARD GAMES

I do love playing many card games with you dear,
Whatever we play, I always win, I've no fear.
But luck must also come into the equation,
Decisions need to be made on each occasion.
There is general excitement of taking part,
And I know you do not mind me winning, dear heart.
Playing cards is a pastime we can share,
Soon immersed, gone for a while are worries and cares.

S Mullinger

A Solemn Purpose

When painting a poem
With a purpose solemn
Choose wondrous hues
For this imbues
It with beauty.
It is the duty
Of all art
This to impart.

M MacDonald-Murray

THE SELECTION

Impossible to prove
The happy guide or rule
Our eyes to gleam or move
Tears when in life's cruel
Or maybe treacherous
Plan our own considered
Not applicable to us
By those that decide or 'erred

The judgement final.
What spark of inspiration
Lights these moments for all
In the general thrall is devastation?
So let some guide now
See the way that simple truths
We may avow
Not numbers in the voting booths.

John Amsden

Family

The best thing has been having a family that is close by
You do not appreciate it until you have cause to sigh
Even if I suffer losses now that cause tears
At least I have had them for more than thirty years
Whatever ill may come,
That is a lot longer than some
It may now be under threat
But having had it for so long, is something
for which I am gratefully in debt
So let us toast the past
And hope what has been good will last
If we can all come through,
Life will not be blue.
I have doubts as to what the future does hold
But at least in the family support I have had, I struck gold
Gradual onset of illness
May make the family's size in future be less
But, so far, I have been blessed.

Sunil Hiranandani

My Leo

Way back in 1960, a Daily Mirror feature
had a gold-plated bracelet with your
star sign on a pendant hanging down,
I sent off for my Leo, received it and was
then the happiest girl in Jarrow Town.

It was my lucky charm with its bright red
stones for eyes,
until I lost it to someone who told me
silly lies.

My boyfriend said when it fell from my wrist,
'I'll fix it for you,' then he disappeared
into the mist.

Without my token, my luck took a dip,
even now I miss it, but I'll have to get a grip.

It's strange when you own something and invest
it with your luck,
that evil fairy follows you, what was his name?
Oh, Puck!

Jean Paisley

WORD OF MOUTH

My favourite thing is to talk,
To waggle and wave 'bout my tongue
I've done it since 'fore I could walk,
Since I was a boy, oh so young.

To talk means to me, oh so much,
It means I can offer compassion.
My words they can feel, they can touch,
And talking is always in fashion.

Talking means we can make peace,
It helps us to go make new friends.
And talking, it will never cease,
Only if mankind, it ends.

Talking means we can hear others,
To help us avoid quiet madness.
And talking means that all our mothers,
Can help us through all pains and sadness.

Yet talking for granted we take,
'Oh shut up' so often we say.
But how many minds would just break,
If in silence they spent every day.

So talking is my favourite thing,
I can speak about all other pleasures,
And if we can speak, we can sing,
To talk is man's greatest of treasures.

Geoffrey Woodhead

Afghan Hound

I say, are you looking in the mirror on my bedroom wall
or are you looking straight out the door?
Can you hear what I'm telling you?
I hope you don't mind me plaiting your hair while I talk
but it is so long and silky, I wish I could do more
I know you know what I'm telling you
even if you don't understand it all
please don't look at me that way with your brown eyes
I don't mean to make you sad
but it's better than banging my head
against a brick wall
I know you can keep a secret
as I've told you loads before
there's just one thing that bothers me
I wish you could talk.

Bonzo

White Bread Sandwiches For Tea

White bread sandwiches for tea
Are better for me
Than I thought.
I ought
To tell the world.

Nicola Barnes

THE WAY OF ALL FLESH

(To Jack)

Out of your mother's womb you came
    Boy or girl, it's all the same
Joy and sadness is yours to bring
    As time and years will bring their sting
From babies to childhood as we grow
    Your mother's love you'll always know
And as our teachers learn and tell
    It's up to you to do things well
You're growing up and now you know
    How your character and personality show
Some day you will do a job of work
    I hope it's yours to never shirk
You could be a doctor or a nurse
    An engineer or a builder too
So if you be good and do these things true
                    you'll never want or be disgraced
    For you have found a goodly place
It's hard to grow up and smile in life
    Because the pace of life today is lots of strife
But keep your honour and respect
    And the Good Lord will do the rest
Some day a family man you'll be
    And you will have a family tree
So as you go and do your best
    The birds in your nest will follow your ways
And you will know the Way of the Flesh
    Has never got you into a mess.

Mabel Houseman

Out Of Season

I shall know that I am old beyond redemption
When I ignore those soaring sounds of hope,
The songs of birds,
Soaring to raise the dead of soul
From contemplation of our doom.

If, like the spokesmen of our older gods,
I could believe the world and all things in it
Were there to give praise and meaning to my race,
I'd understand the joy, against all reason,
Of my new robin's song in winter.

But I who have heard this young bird's grandaddy
Hail the day from the self-same bough
Know the shortness of his breed's creative season,
Threatened by cat and crow.

This is his winter dream of summer idleness
A counterpoint of wonder without wile
To the languid, pointless glory of the butterfly
Weaving its patterns of sunshine.

So let me never curse the cold again.
There will be another summer of the heart:
A time for contemplation without stress,
A pause for creative mindlessness,
My time for exultant - though fortunately silent - song.

Ted Harriott

AURORA

When first I cast my eyes upon you,
so majestic, so resplendent you filled my view.
A vision seen through pockets of windowpanes.
So large and imposing.
I looked up. I looked down and then along. Yet still
unable to survey the picture as a whole.
So near, that I felt to reach out my hand I would
touch you, feel you, caress you.
The hindrance of the glass panes protected you and
prevented this premature intrusion.

That moment eventually arrived.
We departed together and everyone cheered.
How ecstatic we all were.
We were on our way. None of us knew what the
next eleven nights would have in store for us.

There was music, dancing, theatre shows and many
wonderful places to visit. But, I always returned to you.
You felt safe and warm and gave me so many joys.
Like all good things, however, it had to come to an end.
When we returned, I left you, all forlorn.
One final glance over my shoulder and there you were
Still majestic, still resplendent.
To leave you then, was my sad loss. Being with
you had been the best thing in my life.
So, here's to you, Aurora. My ocean liner of the seas.
Until we meet again.

Naomi Donegan

School Dragons

(Baby dragons are given to children as certificates when children do good work)

I go to school nearly every day
I don't go there just to play
I go there to work on my sums
If I get them all right I impress my mum
I like it when we read and write
I dread detention when I get in a fight
When I'm good I earn a baby dragon
When I get home I put them on my wall
I'll believe in them still when I am tall.

Brad Beals (5)

PRECIOUS MOMENTS

The things that I treasure
the most in life,
are:
my husband's company and
love, and
curling up with a
favourite
book or magazine, or
notepad, in
which I shall
write poetry, stories, articles,
or letters,
during the silent hours, whether early
or late,
whilst my husband sleeps,
in the next room,
in our somewhat untidy flat in
Basingstoke, that reflects
our lifestyles and our
characters
so perfectly; the soft
toys that surround me
are the
cream in
my
chocolate
cake, I
suppose. Life is so good!

Paula Puddephatt

AMANDA HORLOCK

The best things in life
Yes, indeed, Amanda Horlock
A most talented actress
One of my favourite actresses is Amanda
Beautiful brown hair and eyes
She is a most excellent actress
Beautiful talented Amanda Horlock
Just some of her stage roles
Mary McGinty in 'Once A Catholic' - excellent.
Fairy Bowbells in 'Dick Whittington' - excellent
Beatrice in 'Commedia dell'Arte - Double Trouble' - excellent
Titania in 'A Midsummer's Night's Dream' - excellent
Constance Neville in 'She Stoops to Conquer' - excellent
Mrs Samsa in 'Metamorphosis' - excellent
Also written, performed and toured in her own solo play
'Advice to a Daughter'
On television she's appeared in
Nurse David in 'The Innocents'
Pearl in 'Over Here'
Barbara Harris in 'The Prostitutes'
Padre and Lisa in 'The Detective'
Amanda Horlock is indeed an excellent actress
Amanda Horlock, star of the future
She is talented and should be a star
One day the name 'Amanda Horlock'
Should be a household name
Yes, Amanda Horlock, a *star*
A most beautiful talented actress
Amanda Horlock, Amanda Horlock!

David J Hall

After The Examinations

It was a fun-packed holiday,
Laughing, screeching, shouting,
Then jostling intruded -
I was knocked down,
Furious, I sat gathering
Enough venom to get even.
Then you handed me nuts;
I looked up and saw you smile,
A huge sunburst of a smile.
It had healing in it.
I was instantly calmed;
I forgot my hurt and my revenge.

Quickly we were being rounded up
For the homeward buses.
You were gone but I was convinced
I'd see you soon: I returned often
To the scene but you were nowhere;
Ten years later I am still awaiting
That vesper smile.

Mary Frances Mooney

CHRISTMAS JOY

Christmas joy.
Gifts of love.
Sent from the heavens
Or from higher above?
My Christmas love to Santa is
A love that brings laughter.
A love that is held in splendour
A love that is cherished and true.
These are the precious gifts of love.
Beauty for all to behold.
Like the power of all eternal.

Colette Breeze

A Special Daughter

Like two sky-blue jewels
Your eyes shone at me.
I held you in my arms thinking,
'How could this be?'

Nine months I was pregnant,
But I could do nothing to prepare
For the love and the joy
That we were going to share.

Your small hands get bigger
A little each day.
It's like I'm watching my childhood
When I see you at play.

Now I know why my mum
Says the things that she says -
The love she feels for her children
Is bigger than immense.

For love is more precious
Than the most precious of jewels;
And the love I feel for you
Has been a liberating tool.

For now I can decide
What's important, you see -
The time we spend together dear daughter,
Is the most special thing for me.

Katherine Lunn

Sunset

Watch
As the sun sets
In the sky.
Everyone says
Goodbye
Twinkling on the sea
How beautiful it can be.

Katya Lunn (7)

THE BEST IN LIFE

The best thing in life
Is love, in its many ways
Lovers in love
Bride and groom in love
Animals love their owners
Fantastic thoughts live with those in love
Yes, the best thing in life is love
And it is completely free.

Alma Montgomery Frank

THE BEST THINGS IN LIFE

Between the covers of a book
The best things in life are found
Choose one, find a quiet space
Life becomes a calmer place
Travel through pages anywhere
From busy cities to mountains bare
The excitement of a thriller
Who done it, who is the killer?
Children transported, eyes alight
Adventure stories, sheer delight
Enter into a world of spies
Where mystery and intrigue lies
On safari or jungle story
Always enthralling, often gory
Expeditions over ice and snow
Mountaineers compelled to go
Catalogues of next year's flowers
Wile away some happy hours
Travel to world-wide places
No passports or heavy cases
A good book, peace all around, is where,
The best things in life are found.

Iris Owen

Scent Of Freedom

No greater fragrance exists,
Than that shared by the flowers of the wild,
Having little need of a scent bottle or large store,
In order to share in their delights

The honeysuckle, the rose,
The heathers of the moorland mountainside,
Each owning a friendship waiting to be shared,
If only, you have the time.

Fresh air, provider of the counter,
Upon which their goods are displayed and served,
And for all, without the need of wealth,
Joy and pleasure, for each and everyone is reserved.

So when wishing to share and appreciate,
    - Life's scents and fragrances -
Search not upon a shelf, hidden within a shop,
Join the flowers in their natural surroundings,
    - In the freedom of the wild -
    - The owners of the many -
Without ever the need of a bottle,
        - with a stopper in the top.

Bakewell Burt

ADONIS

He stood under the waterfall, under the spray,
In shadows I watched, in the water he played,
Looking in wonder, so lean and so tall,
With nothing to hide, my eyes they saw all,
Phallus erect, touched his navel with youth,
Such beautiful wonder, nature's own truth,
I stood in the shadows, a glorious sight,
I could not avert him, try as I might,
Skin glistening wet, his body so lithe,
If only he knew I stood hidden, beside,
An artist could never have painted the scene,
Gushing of water, on his body serene,
A noise and he listened, the water he left,
Coming my way, such a shortness of breath,
My eyes widely opened, he had broken the spell,
In whirlpools of wonder, my soul it now dwells.

W Curran

JOYOUS LIVING

Taking the dogs for a walk
On an early summer dawn,
Aware that this is the best time
Before the heat of late morn.
Having a young grandchild to stay
And knowing he's happy here,
After parting from his parents
Without a single tear.
Inviting a friend for a meal,
Knowing she's now all alone,
Hearing the joy in her voice
As she thanks me over the phone.
Reading a good book at bedtime,
Knowing I'll soon be asleep,
Saying a small, silent, prayer
My safety that night to keep.
My life is full of such joys
These are only a few
But one thing I do know for sure,
The best of them all is you.

Joan Chapman

MAGIC OF LIFE

The best things in life
Are simple and true
Like having a warm tub
When the snow's made you blue

Like feeling the rain
On your face when it's hot
Or tasting sweet nectar
When your gut's in a knot

The best things in life
Include music and song
Kissing and dancing
When your friends come along

Fresh smells from the garden
When it's rained overnight
Howling gales on the outside
When in bed tucked up tight

There are so many things
That make life simply the best
The rub of your pet
On your legs when you rest

Like laughing at jokes
That are told over booze
And going to bed
For an afternoon snooze

The best things in life
Are not hidden from view
So experience the magic
That your senses find you.

Sandra Griesbach

A Beautiful Morning

This is such a beautiful morning
with myriad bird songs, ring
Everything is fresh and new
this makes me feel special too.
Like all good things this can't last
by mid morning all this will pass.
The hustle and bustle of the day
will hold us powerless in its sway
So . . . hold this moment as long as you can
before it is destroyed by noisy man.

Valerie Ovais

My Best Friend

I feel sad as the date draws near,
The day I had to say farewell.
Silently I shed a tear,
For the friend I loved so well.

This friend was everything to me
She never found fault or blame
She was always there just for me
Even when I brought her shame.

My friend to me was like no other
And sorely I do miss her
For she was my own dear mother
And I'd give the world to kiss her.

Chris Cassidy

MY BICYCLE

I love to ride,
I love to glide,
Up and down the country roads,
Narrow or wide;

Feeling the wind,
Upon my face,
With my aim of achieving,
My goal;

To get to the next village,
To do my shopping;

It saves time waiting,
For the buses,
And money too,
And I have a lovely view;

If I could drive,
And had a car,
I would buy,
A cycle rack,
For the back.

Jane Milthorp

Going 'On Line'

I'm not going 'on line',
Without it life is fine.
A life that is real
Has more appeal.
It may not make me wealthier,
But it is certainly healthier:
To go for a country walk,
To meet friends and have a talk:
To see my food before I buy it,
To know it's fresh before I try it:
And; to keep my secrets safe.

I'm not going 'on line',
That decision is mine.
What does your life mean?
You stare at a screen:
Do you know if the sun shines?
Or if the moon has dark lines?
Can you see the blackbird on her nest?
The young hedgehog looking at her best?
Don't you miss the first crocus?
You'll see it out of focus
After you've been staring at the screen.

Catherine Blackett

Our Little Dutch

We once had a rabbit
It was perfect just to show
It was a little chocolate Dutch
We thought we would have a go.

We groomed it and placed it in a pen
Then had a look around
Till it was judging time
What a surprise we then found
Our rabbit was in the last three.

We could not believe it
We thought we hadn't a chance
Against the big breeds there
Especially the Angora, long eared and Belgian hare.

But when ours was chosen
She bit his finger so
We then thought we had lost it
But no, she won, our little doe
The best in all the show.

Maud Sales

My Best Friend

My best friend wears a disguise.
You soon will guess who he is
I surmise.

He is reliable, adoring and always there.
For the trivial things in life he doesn't care.
He does not answer back or disagree,
'Cause I love him and he loves me.

Often he will gaze into my eyes.
Snuggle around my neck with little sighs
Then his purring quite frantic becomes
Like a symphony he vibrates and hums.

Ah, so you have guessed!
He is only a cat
And what use is that?
One of God's more selfish wily creatures
But under all those cat-like features,
It's only at being a cat he does pretend
'Cause really he is my very best friend!

Polly Glenville

JUMP FOR JOY

If I could jump like a kangaroo
I'd come bounding up to you,
I'd sing for joy and share the good news
All about the new life I've found in Jesus!

I'd love you to have it too - oo . . . ooo . . .
It's not just for me, it's for the whole world
To know forgiveness for each guilty stain.
It's like taking a refreshing drink,
Never to be thirsty again!

Jesus has so much to offer,
Yet so many refuse His gift of salvation
Which cost Him His life when He suffered and died
But won for us eternal life when He rose again,
Conquering sin and death and power of Satan.

On Good Friday we remember His death
Giving thanks for the sacrifice He made.
As Easter Sunday dawns we celebrate the resurrection,
The excitement of Mary, Peter and John
Who discovered the empty tomb,
The joyful realisation that Jesus was alive,
Death defeated and salvation won,
Forgiveness made possible through God's Son!

Cathy Mearman

THE GOOD TIMES

We worked and played hard,
No joy was there barred,
We craved it, we bought it,
Not a worry about money, the least little bit.

We could laugh out loud,
Our heart wasn't in a cloud,
Even on a dark day, the sun shone bright,
A smile to our faces it did light.

Abroad on holiday we often went,
To private school our children we sent,
Want a new car, that's no problem,
Just go out have a good look at them.

A grand house we obtained,
As a teacher I trained,
Wealth, happiness and joy,
Were all ours to enjoy.

Never did we think it'd end,
So much grief you would send,
Now to look back brings so much pain,
And we ask, 'Was it all in vain?'

Susan Shaw

Dedicated To The Carers

With caring hearts and a helping hand
The carers are there to understand
For the elderly who cannot walk
A friendly chat, a kindly talk

Long nights on duty always ready to care
Problems to solve or a burden to share
Comfort for those who cannot sleep
A shoulder to cry on for those that weep

Visitors greeted with a cup of tea
Homely and welcoming one has to agree
Every Christmas excitement in the air
Home all decorated with colour and flair

Party time with buffet and drink
Music and singing, folks in the pink
Cards exchanged, raffle to be won
Residents and families all having fun

Extra hours, carers volunteer with a smile
Devotion to the elderly very worth while
So to all you carers old and new
Residents and families say a big 'thank you'.

Brenda M Hadley

LIFE'S FREE GIFTS

The best things in life are always free
Hearing birds singing in a tree
Children laughing at their play
Seeing them skipping another day

A walk in the country to see
Animals running wild and free
Deer, fox and rabbits too
Will help you see the day through

The ripple of a running stream
Fish jumping and mountains gleam
The joy of freedom as you walk
Good conversation as you talk

So please spend your free time
As I often spend mine
Walking our lovely countryside
You really don't want a guide.

Jean Bradbury

SMALL THINGS

The best things in life are often the smallest,
Not the biggest or even the tallest.
When young we can only give,
Tiny things to help another to live.
And yet often these things are cherished most of all,
For they are easily moved as they are so small.
A smile that comes naturally to a face,
Will always add readily to grace.

Betty Green

So Little Can Mean So Much

To my little friends the sparrows,
Sitting in my garden tree.
I watch you line-up, just like soldiers,
Singing happily for me.

Like darts of light, you swoop to earth,
To snatch away the bread,
There is eager anticipation,
When you are waiting to be fed.

I do not grudge this meal of scraps,
It seems a little price to pay
For when I hear the beauty of your song,
The notes inspire me, in a special way.

And once again, we see the love,
From Mother Nature's gentle touch,
As we are constantly reminded,
That so little, can mean so much.

Wendy Adam

My Favourites List

The colour purple
To dance all night long
A tall café latte
Singing a chilled out song
Spending time with my brother
Going shopping with my mum
Chatting with my dad
Sucking my right thumb
Kissing my gorgeous husband
Eating out with friends
Going to the theatre
Making amends
Relaxing in a bubble bath
Reading a good book
Slobbing out on the sofa
Being able to cook
A bright sunny morning
A clear starry night
Lots and lots of favourite things
But most of all to appreciate them,
My touch, taste, hearing, smell and sight.

Lindsey Brown

Best Things Are Free

The best things in life are free,
Once found it never ends,
What could this special gift be?
The gift of Christian friends.

The best things in life are free,
As plentiful as the fresh air,
The mountain that sweeps to the sea,
That God gave to show that he cared.

The best things in life are free,
Our blessings would make a large pile,
What better gift would there be,
Than the magic of a child's smile.

The best things in life are free,
If we openly and willingly embrace,
The gift handed down from that tree,
Christ's unconditional love and grace.

Bill Hayles

Don't Forget

All the best things in life
are what money cannot buy.
A lowering sky on a rainy day,
a rainbow way up high.

Have you searched for the gold
at the end of the bow?
You'll find it where the sunset gleams
and the stars put on their show.

Have you seen a swan rise up
like a lumbering jumbo jet,
or seen the skylark rise and fall
with sweetest song, and yet

wander round the midnight hour
when traffic is more calm,
and hear the nightingale trill out,
that's truly nature's balm.

Houses, cars, material things
we need, all have their place,
but don't forget what makes this life,
what dulls the hassle, slows the pace,
what wonders every day we face,
what takes away the stress and strife,
and makes our hearts sing.

Wendy Ray

Game Cock Inn

Game Cock Inn, food,
About half-way on our walk
Mouth-watering draft Strongbow welcome
Equally, water for the dog.

Cool, clear, refreshing.
On we go rejuvenated.
Cock Wood full of bluebells.
Kick back in our heels.

Inn's hospitality nurtured
Nazareth's with room.
Necessary - basic care.

Robert D Shooter

EPPING FOREST

Spirit of green engendered in liberty
Sweeping across the glanded glades
Tangled tree spirits in tarnished brief
Dancing on shades of sunlit lauded leaves.

Some reveries of buttercups in a sea of grass
Sported squirrels where frolicking en-mass
A listed gesture abbotted in a shallow ditch
Songs of flyers in myrtled melodious pitch.

Conversers of the mind in greenish code
Stimulations of heart in a gentler mode
Spirits of nubile shadows laying aside
Some sultry caresses for the winded bride.

Durlabh Singh

THE BEST THINGS IN LIFE

What are the best things in life?
To each his own, I guess!
For me it's the wonder of nature,
A day passing by without stress.
A letter or visit from family,
Something to give me a smile!
Meeting old friends, unexpectedly,
Whom I have not seen for a while.
A flower grown from tiny seed,
Blossom on trees in the spring,
Squirrels, playing on the grass,
A chorus of birds that sing!
New babies born in the family,
A phone call from somebody dear,
Lights at Christmas, happiness,
Times of goodwill and good cheer!
An achievement, after long trying,
Accomplishing things, worthwhile,
But most of all, the best things in life,
Is seeing a sad person, *smile!*

E M Eagle

Best Things In Life

Oh - what I could do with a lottery win,
Millions of pounds to spend with my kin,
New homes and new cars would do for a start,
Plus fashion galore and fine works of art.
Anxiety and debt would be a thing of the past,
We'd be happy, secure with no worries at last.
But wait, I'm just dreaming, I must think things through,
Would I be happy? Would my friends still be true?
Could a win be the wedge to split my family apart,
Could my happiness change to a crushed, broken heart.
The risk is too great, there's so much to lose,
The ticket is tempting, the time's now to choose,
I've put my money away with a relieving sigh,
What made me decide that I shouldn't buy.
My family is close and they really care,
Be it sad times or happy, we talk and we share,
I'm a daughter, a mother, a sister, a wife,
I've finally realised, I've got the best things in life.

M McDonald

HUSBAND

I was never perfect, did not profess to be
The only thing I was certain of, is that I was me.
Made up of hands and arms and legs, every vital part,
That is how you saw me, when you gave me your heart.

Do I look the same to you? I ask myself inside,
Or do you see me now as someone who should hide?
I know the love you gave me, will always be the same,
As it was the day I said 'I do' and took your name.

I don't know how to thank you for what my life has been,
The many things you do for me, most of them unseen.
I could never wish for any other one than you
And so I confess you are my love, my whole life through.

Letitia Snow

IN THERE SOMEWHERE

It's that thought within, floating -
Incomplete with others of the mood,
Which hangs about the boughs of words,
Not forming, but fostering a benevolence -
A propensity to approve, a willingness to like.

Finding a beauty spot in an old sandstone wall,
That certain blush, yet a blush hardly worth the mention.
That combination in the coursing,
Coursing like all the rest, yet differing
By the measure of the indefinable.

In there somewhere is the ingredients
To please the eye, excite self to appreciate
And remember the hands, the ideas -
Incarnate of the rustic trade,
Which transcends the drudge
Of its daily rituals.

The floating half-thought
That hangs about the boughs
Of limbs and minds, fostering,
Creating beauty spots.

Alex Laird

SEB

He came one sunny morning
The sky was all aglow
His tail was wagging madly,
I knew I'd love him so.
We travelled fields and valleys,
Saw mountains covered in snow,
Always together trudging to and fro.
How the years passed quickly
Five years, seven, ten,
Our life together was special even then.
Things don't last forever,
The dreaded day came,
I lost the dearest friend
Life's never been the same
I think of him in heaven
Running down a lane
Watching over me
Till we meet again.

Edie Glen

DOUBLE LOVE

For those who haven't got them,
They're really missing out,
The best things ever in my life
Are these, without a doubt.

Granddaughters - double trouble,
Double hugs and double love,
Double sunshine when I'm down,
Double blue skies up above.

Double laughter, double giggles,
Double cuddles oh so tight,
Double daydreams when I'm lonely,
Double sweet dreams every night.

Double, 'I love you Grandad,'
Double, 'What shall we play?'
Double, 'Take us to the park,
The sun is out today.'

I'm in my second childhood,
They've made me young again,
And when my joints and muscles ache,
I wouldn't dare complain.

They've made my life so special,
My heart just bursts with pride,
When I go out walking,
With 'double darlings' by my side.

Jim Sargant

The Apple Tree

At summer's close
With apples red
The apple tree
Bends down her head

We pluck the fruits,
Lay them in store -
The tree throws up
Her head once more.

November and December blow
Into the New Year's drifting snow
Which bends hard down
The apple boughs.

Then out we go
And shake them free,
Up lithely springs
The apple tree.

And in the failing afternoon
Into its twigs
A robin flits
And red as any apple sits.

Terry Smith

JIGSAW OF LIFE

It's time for reminiscence
A new year has begun.
It's time to fill those spaces
To scan the years long gone.

You take your box of treasures
And then take off the lid.
You look at all the pieces
To see what is within.

You fumble with the pieces
And don't know where to start.
Your mind goes back and further back
And now you're in a spin.

You find a treasured photo
A wallet or a purse.
A pretty golden necklace
And all have little worth.

But, the people they belonged to
Were special in your life.
You loved them very dearly
And miss them without doubt.

It hurts to look inside that box
But look inside you must.
Without these little treasures
Your life I think would rust.

So, don't despair of loved ones' gone
Just keep the precious treasures.
As you look back with tearful eye
Your life's enriched forever.

J Mary Kirkland

CHILDHOOD MEMOIRS

Remembering back to your childhood days.
Way back where there were no worries
Climbing trees, knock up ginger, bubble gum and handstands
Swapping stickers for the latest magazine
Skateboards, bike rides and secret clubs
Running to school always late
Giggling in class, daydreaming out of the window
Can't wait to get home and play with friends, watching the school clock
Saturday morning cartoons, the old corner shop
Remember when everyone in your street spoke to each other
And nobody was prettier than your mum
Summer holidays that go on forever
The old ice cream van that plays a tune
Grass camps, river trips and warm summer nights
The latest yo-yo craze, water balloons and play fights
Getting a foot of snow was a dream come true
Remember when going into town or the park was really somewhere!
Sherbet dips, hop scotches and double dare
Friends staying over, midnight feasts and staying up late
Having a best friend and keeping secrets
Parties and piggy backs, laughing until your sides hurt
Sports all day, never tiring, ruff and tumble with Dad
Getting 25p was considered decent pocket money
If you remember some or all of these memories then you have lived
Taking you back in time;
For those of you who need a rest from the adult life.

Claire Nicole

Why Do I Run?

I run and become one
My mind and body working in unison
Taking me forward, heading towards my goal
Somewhere out there on the horizon . . .
There is a pounding in my heart
And sometimes my head and aching legs
Ask the question 'Why did I start'?

There are so many unexplored places to see
Many of them only a mile or two away.
Running through my favourite wood
Somehow the seasons conspire
To change a familiar view
I know this track so well
But there's always something new

So after the miles are done
And I'll have the satisfaction
My personal battle has been won
Soon I will catch my breath and
Join back into this busy world a little bit calmer

So when friends ask my why?
I'll just reply . . .
'Why don't you give it a try?'
Not many of them will,
It is easier in this multimedia world
To seek a less demanding thrill.

Steve Smithson

VOAR

Spring is round the corner the season of lengthening light
when we can say in good belief, goodbye to winter's weary night
the soon profuse romance in nature's blink
a letter-love for plant and life to think
the early snowdrop still, in last year's leaves
and scratching birds like scoundrels in the eaves
your neighbour too is out and the farmer is about
as there amongst his sheep you hear him shout
the burn now in flood is full of first run trout
dream on boy, with luck you take one out.

J M Heddle

BLUEBELLS ON THE HILL

Bluebells, bluebells, bright and blue,
May I come and visit you?
If I'm careful where I tread
Not stepping on a single head,
May I come and sit quite still
To where you spread across the hill?
Smell your perfume with a smile
From my seat upon the stile?
You flower briefly then you're gone,
But in my mind you linger on.
Dark winter days I think of you,
Close my eyes and see your blue
Swathed across that springtime hill.
In my thoughts, I hold you still.
Next springtime, bluebells, bright and blue,
May I return and visit you?

Haidee Williams

WINTER'S END

Daffodils stinted because of the frost,
  snowdrops are limping, but all is not lost,
the sun is returning and warming the earth,
  soon grass will be growing for all it is worth.

Hedges are turning to purplish bloom,
  leaves are now forming and will be out soon,
lambs in the fields with their mothers who watch,
  tractors leave fields, on the road there's a botch.

Days getting longer soon March will be here,
  clocks put on forward, that will give me a cheer,
cricket soon starts and then will come rain
  and our season continues all over again.

Cherry trees blooming, a sight of delight
  heralds the end of the long winter night,
march winds will blow causing blossoms to fall
  Easter soon with us, then traffic will crawl.

Leslie Holgate

FALKA

You're there when I need a friend,
With a love that will never end.
You're that special something in life,
My partner in a world of strife.
You're that sparkle in my eye,
That makes me want to try.
To see what you see.

You're like the breaking of dawn,
On that special day you were born.
You're like that child within us all,
Memories of youth we recall.
You're like the smile on my face,
With elegance and grace.
I see what you see.

You're the truth within my heart,
A bond that will never depart.
You're a flame that burns through the night,
Eternal ray of hope and light.
You're an angel to my sleep,
A friend I wish to keep.

Amanda Jayne Biro

To Offer Love

The best in life
Is giving to another
Everyone suffers strife
Folk feeling better
When receiving grace
For each day to face

A lovely feeling
To offer love
Given with meaning
As from heaven above
There is no doubt
When one is about

To each of us
There comes upset feeling
One filled with sorrow thus
A helping hand is appealing
A blessing in disguise
From one so wise

One gains fulfilment
In their own life too
When showing sentiment
For a heart to soothe
Bringing one bliss
Not to be missed.

Josephine Foreman

SUMMERTIME

Warm balmy nights,
And hot summer days
I think of you as I sit in the shade
With ice cold tea, a good book and
A seat in a sunny glade.
Days filled with joy and family fun,
Or just sitting on a beach enjoying the sun.
Exploring the castles, the valleys, the lochs,
Family picnics, tennis and quoits,
Then ice cold beer and a feeling of cheer,
As the sun dips slowly into the night sky.

Sue Peach

FRUIT FLAVOURED WORDS

The apple harvest is complete
and the wind sighs through the apple trees
shadows move around the orchard
I retire to my window seat
deaf and blind to the outside world

I admire the scarlet fruit display
upon a silver plate
as happy as a lark
I step inside my favourite book

The old book is edged with gold
but means more than gold to me
it brings forth fruit year after year
just like the apple tree.

I swallow slowly and digest
the clever cryptic words
they leave me like the apples
with a rosy hue
and dreams of poetical works
as smooth as apple juice.

Some of the pages are dog-eared
adding charm to the age
each time I pick it up
I find a friend on every page

With this treasure I would not part
no matter what
I travel through the chapters
with a happy heart.

Beth Anderson

FRIENDS

These most of us have many kinds,
Some with very intellectual minds,
Our friends we choose,
And wouldn't want to lose.

They share in our troubles and joy,
We also have moments when they annoy
True friendship stays the course,
Loyalty is also very staunch.

People have friends all over England,
Many writing letters by hand,
Some we are in reach and often see,
To have friends how happy it can be.

Pamela Earl

A LIFE WORTH LIVING

'This is your marrow
- look - you can see -
I've carved in small letters -
your name - our Betty.'

'When you get older -
you'll have your own patch -
you can grow what you like
with flowers that will match.'

This was my father -
who loved the outdoors -
trees, fruit and flowers -
and lovely rose bowers.

I remember his Morgan -
the first car in the street -
and drives out in the country
our grandmother to meet.

Quiet country lanes,
- yes - at a slow pace;
time to see the beauty -
(not like today's mad
    motorways' race!)

Organic vegetables?
- Of course! He loved the good earth;
blackcurrants and apples -
- our inheritance from birth.

And now - after decades
we are learning again
to respect Mother Nature,
and that we do not labour in vain.

The rewards that we reap -
as my parents knew well,
are from what we put in -
and gain us either heaven
or hell!

Beatrice Wilson

Good Music

Whenever I am alone and free,
I put on music as loud as I can.
For me this is my favourite thing,
And I do it every day at every given chance.
Good tunes and fast music *forever.*

Rajeev Bhargava